Fort Not

Emily Skillings

The Song Cave

Published by The Song Cave
www.the-song-cave.com
© 2017 Emily Skillings

Gestation (Birthing in Madripore) by Steven Arnold, 1984.
© The Steven Arnold Museum and Archive.

Design and layout by Janet Evans-Scanlon

ISBN: 978-0-9967786-9-5
Library of Congress Control Number: 2017945847

FIRST EDITION

for John, for David

"It is a false wall, a poet: it is a lying word.
It is a wall that closes and does not."
—LAURA (RIDING) JACKSON

Table of Contents

Backchannel

I buy an orb-shaped glass orb
and a designer candle
and go home to touch myself.

Take off everything but my shag coat,
turn on some minimalist drone
sent to me by a man.

I was never almost partly there.
I was on a stone beach in Newfoundland
enjoying near-perfect sound
with the early, hovering crowd of bodies.

I was in early evening Brooklyn
backchanneling an elder about acupuncture
receiving dull, potato-shaped aches,
age-old pricks, hyperbolic
Encyclopedia of World Mythology-sized feelings.

Ereshkigal bolts the seven gates of the underworld
against her sister, ruler of heaven.

Isis buries replicas of Osiris's genitals
in Egypt's maternal earth fields.

Some chick gets pregnant when she squats in clay.
Her baby a limbless waterpot with a giant mouth
betrays her in the river.

A glitter splotch moves across my eye.
Bacteria raft?
I've been drinking too much possessed broth.
I pre-condition. I condition. I deep condition.
I leave-in condition. I deflect an image
of the body as a series
of hermetically sealed plastic cubes
filled with sluggish wasps.

I can skillfully point at something
by connecting it to a term
with a little line from my
character viewer of recently
used icons, but really there's nothing
in these texts to end on.

I climb out into a thought—
some rare embossed urn,
youngish flowers pasted
on the back of light,
misaligned polka dots
on an entitled seam,

a pulse in my ass,
the exquisitely dropped beat
I've been searching for
in most holdable objects.

Garden of Slow Forms

In the middle of your life it is a Sunday.
Shocked blossoms rush, network, embed freely.

You decide to take your new throat for a walk
And track a softening center ring of thought.

The daylight is scrolling itself to death.
Everything presses into an atmospheric parfait.

Objects held by mounds of soil
On-and-off themselves in neat rows.

The available openings open wider-open.
Slits, in bunches, grow wild terminals.

A lake explodes in a nearby district.
A heavy storied treeline stores a form.

Instrument of indecision, the Calabash harp,
Combs into a cream-colored fog.

Matron of No

There are so many paintings of Lucretia
stabbing herself and they're all
pretty terrific. My personal favorites
are the ones where she looks bored (Rembrandt,
Parmigianino, Sellaer, Cranach
the Elder) like she's just sticking
a casual reminder
between her tits that life is suffering,
and a certain quota of daily blood
is needed for a decant into that ancient
ceremonial chalice of feminine shame. Drip

drip. Reclining on a sofa in the mid-century style
I allow a stranger's black-and-white boy cat
with bright pink rubber caps on all its claws
and a clipped tail to knead a soft space, this shelf
of fat above my organs. It feels invasive
but not unpleasant, a therapy
taken in foggy discomfort.

Caught in my phone's own beam
is my greasy face, which, downturned,
admires the Expressionist skyscraper
proposed but never built
by Ludwig Mies van der Rohe

for Berlin's Friedrichstraße, its points
pointing at an overgrowth in me,
my finger hovering over the street,
no vehicles below, no people,
the black smudge of city movement
implying by erasure
those who move through
its striated, dynamic soot.

And what of the top? A blade garden.
Full of women seeking aesthetic revenge.
I think I might like to go away.
I think I might like to bond
with the darkest stuff, revisit the peeling corner
that exists in almost every room
and is exquisite artwork that nobody looks at—
to sit with it awhile until a feeling of lateral
motion takes over, a whisk
into a syncretion of senses
from different legendary themes.

And now the cat is on the dining room table
licking goat cheese from an earthenware bowl.
The big windows let the night in on a timer.
The room does its thing to me again.
"Your lips / your eyes." That gentle shuffle
of petals across the brain.

Nine Times out of Ten You're Not Ablaze

it was the smallest world

mistakes in the eye made a pattern breathe

a range where phenomena multiply

the big bright sign on the sky wasn't thereforeable

when I looked at the wall of books I came apart

your nothing pressing down on mine

I think something clever was asked earlier

re: sprawl, allover glimmer

true, H was an ancient nerve destroyer

and I borrowed this line from a glass bank

windows reflecting porches onto roads

here spat my punk ancestor

and to the writers listed below I dedicate my vast

natural shapes, unnatural ones

just a little break here

no reason

you don't need any reason

When I Was a Glacier

That Breughel painting
of hunters returning
in winter, the filmmakers
go nuts for it. A sad rabbit
on a stick & more. It's like
really in there, tonally—
a male, disappointed
group trudge towards
a more lighthearted
communal flurry, women
and children full of fire
upholding weird roofs
doing the *real* work.

A moment ago, I moved
something (not particularly
large) to the other side
of the table and felt
so old and immense
and in control. Like a truck
crunching on its path.

I project white onto the
floorboards. And isn't it
this music from that ballet
that always makes us?
Indistinguishable
from a folktale pink shock

of pure quartz through the wall.
Give me one irregular mark
for my thigh to pit the year
against. 16th-century sound
gets all over the daybed
and you relocate your teeth
to the opposite nipple.
My thought in that moment
it's a brutal cave.
Brightest bird, tailfeather,
increasing gray line, fail me
my distant mountain.

Baby Food

I ate some.
It tasted fine.
I'm alive.
Blood is coursing
through my veins.
I could call out
into darkness—
I could harness
some powers
beyond my
usual scope
of action.
I feel fortified
and nutrient-
rich. I think
the baby food
did this
to me. It was
banana squash, two
things I've never
thought to
combine. Who are
these brilliant,
innovative

chefs we appoint
for our youth?
How long
will I feel this way?
I don't have
a baby (I'm
ambivalent about
mothering), but
I've always
really wanted
to publicly breastfeed
something. Ideas?
I want to drape myself
and also to expose
my feeding breasts,
and argue about my right
to expose or not expose
those feeding breasts.
I want to get in fights
with other breastfeeders
and non-breastfeeders
on the internet
and in person.
In the park.
In the coffee shop.
To come
to blows.

I would get
that special pillow,
the bra
with the holes
in it,
pumping freely
into containers
of many sizes.
I want to yell
from a bathroom stall,
"Would *you* want
to eat lunch in here?!"
I want to judge men for staring.
I want to judge men
for looking away,
to be equally
frustrated and empowered.
I'd feed my lover
and my friend
as much milk
as they wanted,
one on each side,
more than a baby
could take.
They'd spread on
that special
anti-chafing ointment.
I'm thinking about leaking

onto a rag,
or a document,
moistening a
territory.
The areola,
that bobbing
spot on
the GPS.
Nipple kinesphere.
It's so powerful
to have food in you
streaming somewhere
or just out.
The sun dips
below the equator.
The smallest,
rubberized sensation
broke my personal
barrier. I'm not
even thinking now,
just acting—
pure, unbridled
physical being.
I feel like I'm talking
extremely loud. Would
you say that
is accurate?
It's a Monday

in America.
I'm 26 years old.
Could you help me
with my body?

Siege of La Rochelle

The first thing to know about running across the battlefield is that if she's not relaxed, she's not going to enjoy it.

One of the most important things you can do at this point is read her battlefield—and by that, we mean monitor her ammunition levels and pay attention to how she's moving her infantry. If you're doing something she likes, you'll notice that the battlefield raises and lowers. You really need to learn how to listen to her bloody, massacred acres. If you're not sensitive to how she's responding, you might as well be off in the corner with your bayonet, soaking in the blood.

Don't be afraid of breaking out the heavy artillery. It can be an invaluable tool to the art of the battlefield. The average woman takes 20 minutes to advance, so you're going to be there for a while. Use something small and easily handled so you can still feel like you're in control of the battlefield.

Compliment the battlefield.

Talk to the battlefield in the morning and tell her you're going to pamper and tease her all night and give her an epic bloodbath.

Locate her throughout the day. Signal her violent things.

Tell her you love her or at least that she's important to you.

Give her a gift. Anything. If the gift is delivered to her in front of her troops, you win.

Dress for success, and wear plenty of Mylar or chainmail.

Create a romantic environment that engages as many of the senses as possible. Use drones, cryptography, erotic surveillance, aromas, chemical gas, and make sure the bodies are cleared away afterwards.

Give her a full battlefield massage.

"The buildup should be like a crescendo. You need to start increasing pressure and increasing speed. Some like a side-to-side tactical motion in the fracas, while others prefer an up-and-down pummeling rhythm," says Somoza.

Some will be more into the public beatings and others will be more into enforced disappearances. Judge your movement based on her response. But—and here's the disclaimer—she may not always be victorious. It's not a reflection of your ability.

"Don't be so goal-oriented and caught up in your own ego," Somoza advises.

Your only goal should be to make her feel historical.

One of the greatest things about the battle is when nobody is satisfied and everyone dies.

I Love Wiping My Dirty Hands
on Other People's Things

It has always been the case
a pleasure I action
a small protest I smear
my dirt redistributing
as I cross over to the East Side
hands building
a serum out of the day
I wipe mayo onto microfiber
car seat makeup to
underside of heather gray
couch, into that damp
fresh hotel white
excess lotion on a colleague's
ottoman upholstered
in damask roses
something you put in me
gets painted on eggshell walls
I polish the side
of your mouth
with a greased thumb
thinking of how
when John Cage studied
architecture, he would
carefully rub oil

from his face
into tiny wooden boxes
he'd fitted
a silver pool gathers
somewhere low and bratty
in me and seeps outward
I know I own all this
the way the Overcup
Oak claims the ground
the sloping windshields, the
slow-moving residents
with resinous, sticky dust
in Boerum Hill I apply
my friend's $100 whipped
Brise Marine
white and cold as rabbit fur
in its porcelain tub
ignore the little plastic spatula
designed to discourage
the contaminated
hand from intruding
I dip the pads of three fingers
waves of ancient minerals
crash across my face
I smell like a new coin
the cream is not the same for it
tomorrow I'll be whisked
into the corners of her eyes

as I walk down the stairs
fingers attending
to the folded Band-Aid
that has adhered to itself
in my back pocket, old brown
blood like a token
the tea grows stronger
I have infected the air
around my house
with my house's cake
if you teach me to behave
out there in the grids
and ways I will pluck a hair
from my filthy head and place it
in your mouth

Phoenicia, Hunter, Cairo

for Dorothea Lasky

On the bus ride
from New York to Delhi
I see a dead horse

(at least I think it's dead) laid flat
in a field. The man in front of me
eats Fritos and wears cologne.

I think the real dream
would be to never again
have to beg for sex. To be bent

over a pile of recalled dental chairs.
I recline in my seat. The window takes
hundreds of pictures for me.

The temperature
today so comically low
it's a song.

The Four Causes

Let me backwards into it. Move, that is.
Uncoming towards a bank of eager foam
looped into being by repeat water, repeat
impurity, beaten as if the thing that just happened
just happened in a kind of reclaimed pine air.

No actual reveal—a grind, a year in bits
inside a silo. Reason enough for forgetting.
What did the art do? It settled for itself. It tackled
a bit of maritime scenery, called on a friend.
It glowed its indicators in celery green.

Unfolding drama: A girl or speck goes to a pool
or amphitheater. *Girl or speck* is the material
or matter. *An amphitheater or pool* is the form
or shape the material or matter enters. *Human
uncertainty* is the end. *Stain* is the effect

that finishes it. Did I remember that correctly?
The pre-owned, gently used shelves reverberate
with historical sound. It gets all unsung, enormous.
If I could be unbuttoned, it could be moments ago
when I am all out of the brass in myself.

Flower Chamber

Empty and half awake,
I met my exchange cousin for the first time,
found her services to be almost reliable,
rode the repeating pause to the very top of feeling.

I came, waited, contemplated almost nothing,
was forced to leave after nobody showed up
to the mouth-to-mouth party.
It was almost an hour ago to the second.

It's like those circulated myths about imperceptibly small
yet incredibly dense objects sinking
through an entire apartment complex, five or eight
consecutive living room floors,
to hover in the basement's single bulb.

I'm coming to a curve in this logic.
The line flows itself into a chamber shape
only to swerve, douse my walking project
in ground stimulants, and dissolve.

I walked past the middle-class nausea
of patchy, poorly seeded lawns,
walked into the depressed shopping mall
where each item gets its own store, price tag,

and uniformed guardian, past the woman
who was hurled forever into public,
who dies each day in her own footprints.

I walked and imagined a dock into permission.

I walked up to a building
that advertised a Flower Chamber
of insurmountable beauty on its glass façade.

Between my feet I saw a cobblestone,
and on that cobblestone was a small gold placard,
and on that small gold placard was an engraving.

It read: Here, Right Here
Nowhere Else
Underneath and Above
This Building
Apartment Building Building
Building Avenue
Building Area, Still Building

Building Building Building

Building Building

A New Sound

Oh it was morning and
the city broke,
and along the edges of its fissures
grew a soft, feltlike substance.
Somehow, too, it was a sound.
Not one I could hear, but one I knew was there,
like the drone bookending a breath
and the full plushness of pause
combining into tone.
It waved

    —much like grass waves, but not quite. This is as close
    as I can come without harming an idea of it—

protecting the painful parts
of the city's fresh wounds
from the harshness of the air.

Many citizens were collecting scrapings
in glass tubes, some were smelling it
or rubbing it into their skin.
Lucy, across the deep divide
that now ran through the square,
claimed it had demonic properties.

To me, it felt kind and fresh,
and I noticed a new lightness in people
as they spoke to each other about it
and what it was
and what it would do.

I bent down,
recorded it on my device,
heavy and silver in my right hand.
I touched it with my left

     —the one with the swelling around the smallest nail,
     caused by repeated picking at the site,
     an anxious habit I'd quarantined to one finger—

and some of the sound came off
on the crepe material of my dress.

Bluish smear of soft filings
heralding the unknown,
a prelude buried in its texture.

I returned home, taking the longest route
along a new northeast crevice.
The sun seemed closer than usual.
Light tumbled down buildings

—how we love in the Capitol
is often, I thought, determined
by vectors, ratios, scarcity,
fumes, colors, pockets of air.

I may not even see "you,"
"you" whom I may come to love
and do not yet know,
if how we spend our pay,
if how we make our wages,
is not predetermined to be connected,
and the points where we make our daily stops
fail to become intersections
that collect to form a field of relation—

I plugged my device
into an even larger device
to download the file,
put on my headphones,
pressed play,
turned the sound up.

At first, nothing.
Then, horns ascending in layers,
stepped gardens of strings.
I could hear shifts in the pelvis
around the bow's movement,

the muffle of moss and dirt
and the shoots breaking through them.

It's a new time, I thought,
as I texted my friend
in the other district,
"We're in a new time!"

    —imagining briefly the potatoes
    I'd bought, collected in the cool dark
    of their drawer, how
    they might never again
    be exposed to light—

The recording continued,
but a new sound took its place in me,
a converging of voices
weaving
on the lowest setting.

It went something like this:

We don't want to go to work anymore
We don't want to go to work anymore
We don't want to
don't want to go

And something within me

    —or perhaps directly behind—

began to sing alongside it:

I don't want
I don't want to go
I don't want to go to work
I don't want to work
anymore to go
anymore, anymore

Shoprite

Like dead fish positioned
On a shaved ice incline
Mouths agape towards some vast white space
I am curving muscular spines
Towards the monger of this century
I will not let him, or anyone
Take their eyes off mine
My eighteen cold, wet eyes

One Hundred and Fifteen Palaces

. . . some are courts of serene stone, / Some the civil structures of a war-like elegance as bridges, / Sewers, aqueducts and citadels of brick, with which I declare the fact / That your nature is to vanquish.

—F.T. PRINCE

Get in your bestiary
Get in your magenta clemency
Get in your Americanisms
Get in your preseason lounging suite
Get in your deep shit
Get in your dribble economy
Get in your presidential bubble bath
Get in your rocky mountain high
Get in your encasement of solid blood
Get in your forbidden city

Get in on the copper lightning of a cheek
Get in on the seductress convention
Get in on the recovery threshold
Get in on the misty collective breath
Get in on the chlorophyll spectrum depository
Get in on the mating patterns of gulls
Get in on the greater sense of antelope
Get in on the digital dumpsite

Get in on the getting it on
Get in on falling from boulder to mouth

Step into the sun room
Step into the sensation of gulping sunny delight
Step into the fire of the throat
Step into the only accessible memory
Step into the only accessible memory of running
Step into the collection of antique cookie tins
Step into the bower of painted waves
Step into the metal pail and act predictably
Step into the word by the way it is mispronounced
Step into the volume with watery feet

Arrive at a field housed in the center courtyard
Arrive in the alcove dedicated to tree peepholes
Arrive at the parking space for hoverers
Arrive at the toolbar plugin shed
Arrive at the arena of competitive navel-gazers
Arrive by twilight with the scent rubbings of indigenous stems
Arrive by the tropisms of your ancestors
Arrive as a moviegoer in a blindingly bright theater
Arrive at the truth that your fingers will never relax
Arrive at your fraudulence in a field of mums

Go to sleep in the language of your country
Go to sleep in the circumference of woodwind ceremony

Go to sleep in the warmth of science
Go to sleep alone
Go to sleep with many stuffed animals facing the wall
Go to sleep, but make it a happening in your shawl
Go to sleep to the sound of mechanical emissions
Go to sleep on the strawberry-red carpet, redder than any strawberry
Go to sleep and catch no fish
Go to sleep. The designated resting hours evaporate

Wake up in the wiry miasma
Wake up and accost the Duchess
Wake up inside a cardboard plot
Wake up and tongue the micro-climate of your own mouth
Wake up and aim at glass figures in the Pistol Zen Hall
Wake up! There's no more green in this joint
Wake up and amend the window situation
Wake up in the deep blue pools of your kidneys
Wake up in three consecutive waves
Wake up and start and collapse and regenerate

Whisper across the oaky song sauna
Whisper across authentic jars of poison
Whisper across the sister society of ear-piercers
Whisper your imitations of nesting men
Whisper specific landmarks on the property line
Whisper into the dancing bags of artichoke fat
Whisper into the freaky, scaly depths
Whisper into the boning socket

Whisper into the unless
Whisper. Or don't. Adjust the dial.

Turn a corner to find your leisure waiting
Turn a corner and smell the blooming fields of lavender money
Turn a corner by rotating your favorite spinal column
Turn a corner down on the drifty sheets
Turn a corner in your palace of scratched white slabs
Turn a corner; the fish market is closed on Tuesdays
Turn a corner as you swim the Blue Whale artery
Turn a corner to covet the darkened meat
Turn a corner in your maze of giddy ghosts
Turn a corner. You are here too early

From a distance you notice your lover in a box
From a distance you first glimpse the evangelism factory
From a distance you watch the house build itself
From a distance you call out to the lowering language
From a distance you anticipate the feeling of a snake in your boot
From a distance you finger the discarded swatches
From a distance, imagine her cultivated pile of infomercial
From a distance, create a vacuum seal
From a distance, squint into a den of caged weepers
From a distance, purchase your last lick

A place for nothing, just hanging around
A place for smearing the clay walls
A place to collect the manuals

A place for meditating with an open asshole
A place for tipping the goddamned vats
A place for grinding the insects to powder
A place for your chalkboard lessons
A place where there's always juice in the fridge
A place to name things after your old things
A place exists where nobody does this

Maria Callas

My sinus is a chamber
in which small bells
wave each other songs.
The glass water bottle
   with the mint latex sleeve
     holds the time it takes
to manipulate a window
       into the art I want for
       lunch. I read and reread
the story and still it was
      strange to me, like leaves
        on a tree birthing great birds.
The color came from
        a crushed bug to be
           brushed on the face
of the impostor. Her
        rosy halo disturbed
           the garden's symmetry.
The untranslatable word
        is the heretofore unknown
          room in your house
that presents itself in dreams
        and holds amazing lamps
          and sitting surfaces

you never knew you missed
             out on. It's true—I'm a poem
                      person not book person.
And I never listen to the radio,
             though sometimes its attending
                      sensation surrounds me
suddenly, like a mothering fog
             or a cell of glass tile
                      like a minor spell.

Parts of a World

for Jane Freilicher

light blue above
conversing colors of pre-work
you are inside
a precarious slant
night curtains keep you
in hidden surface arrangements
it's really going to happen soon
and you go

a dark square in his chest
a pretty menacing lean
if not for all the color
turquoise diagonals
attack the doorframe
and a mint cheek

the other shape of intention
threaded candy trees
not bleeding but exploding
a field with an incident on top

these ones come a lot to be against things
their ghosts will hang back
and the turpentine is sad
and wants to coat your nostrils
to touch you
do you like this bit, this part?
what kind of pink are you?

flesh bay curvature
everything in it is herself
plucked trees
into sidelong gaze

you look comfortable
in your grass aura
my brother in leaning

gray dome in blush clutter
your specialized
transparent face
some distant
but not-too-distant era
hanging on
I can't have it, and this makes me
shivering and dark

an exercise of viewing the world
as a table
in mythic proportions
orchid light on cellophane
buildings with steps, with tic-tac-toe grids
three sardines on a plate
surrounded by clouds
what could be better than that?

my silver platform into day
into myself reflected
the classic inside/outside conversation
given new ~~color~~
window, frame, my scaffold, my mirror,
how so many rectangles
form a brain knot

boiled egg porthole into
the memory of a greenhouse
the petals all line up for naming
tapwater waterline splits
the ocular stem
Martian interior calm

on the 22nd day of spring
the sea turned orange
stock characters alighted on billboards
the dunes turned geometry

I'll be inside on my slate
waiting it out
white puffs in a vessel
held very close

blinking hard into seascape
streaming surface
matte neon
out of the corners of ladies'
mouths a feeling
like layers
or years

the traditional attitude
had a sharp, gorgeous tooth
a tone to make your hands ache
clever buildings matching up their seams
the even cleverer Hudson
staying out of the blue business
white megaphones play music
and suck up a little more water

there is the sill
this we notice
then the city
draped torso sizing up a container
then the skyish mountains
blending, conversing
comparing shapes
yellow coming straight
from the source
of all yellow

close your eyes and think
of your favorite painting by Jane Freilicher.
let it rest on the inside of your eyelids
count to 10
(count)

now open your eyes and project that painting
onto the walls of the Parish Hall
at the Poetry Project of St. Mark's Church
on this day, December 12, 2014

Holland Tunnel

so thinking/ About that organism, I disappeared/ Into it
—ALICE NOTLEY

Somewhere there is a hole
waiting for you

to put yourself into it—
hand over the fat of you

(gently, slowly)
into its dark center

until you are a single raw
rod, an inner finger

pointing at a tree you spotted
on the road and think you like.

On the screen that still
somehow holds to magic

an elegant starlet approaches
along a terrifying curve.

Microbes return
minerals to the soil

as you walk to the mall
to abandon your edges.

Sometimes and all the time
you are shut out of days.

You pull the single hair
out of your mouth to achieve sound.

You lose the language necessary
to corrupt a field. And beyond

the factory, what little you have left
spirals into a self-lubricating dawn.

The nearly spoken root
sucks up more water.

The men are vicious pupils
who open and close our springtime.

Little buds everywhere. *I don't get it*
you say, *I don't get it at all.*

You ask a sudden recognition
on the fox-colored sofa

as signals come out from their dens
to arouse you.

You emerge clean, a convinced ball
no claims / no devices.

The room maneuvers and becomes
large. You lean towards the mirror

for hours, manipulating
tiny gardens in your face.

Canary

I held my canary out for you when you said your canary
    felt a little droopy.

Your canary was a ruby drop in my frosty glass of canary.

The canary between us grew for many days.

I wanted to fight the canary, but you held me back.

The officer shot the unarmed canary on a canary I used to
    walk down every day.

When you touched the canary underneath my knee, a
    balloon filled with canary in an eastern corner.

The sound of unmarked canaries overhead frightened the
    rural hospital.

The president has never commented publicly on the
    controversial canary program.

Can you remember where that canary was that we tried
    so many years ago?

Oh, that canary feels so good—just like that.

The canaries carry electricity to our houses in even
    smaller canaries.

When the activists passed out yellow canaries I took one
    and read it.

A canary is born every 8 seconds.

I log onto the large canary to check how my canary
    is faring.

When I go to the supermarket, I check the codes on the
    canaries to make sure they are not genetically
    modified canaries.

Many canaries suffer.

She pressed a thumb into my muscle and all the canary
    was released into me.

When I went outside I saw the sky, it was filled with
    canary.

You held the canary up to my face. You vibrated the
    canary at a new frequency.

You said the best time for canaries was 11:30 am.

The Banks

Lately I've been thinking about how I might like to write
a series of poems as single, unbroken lines that extend far
beyond the borders of any screen or page, penetrating
rightspace as far as they need to in order to magnetize
and attract their particular streaming content and shape.
I say "shape" knowing full well that lines would be line-
looking, but imagining that they (through careful shifts of
rhythm, word length, and elliptical construction maneuvers)
could somehow *curve, pool,* or *orbit* their way out of
predetermined linearity, like a perpetually self-revising river
bank or algal bloom forming via the scrolling and gathering
straightway. In this way, an augmenting line becomes
a walk along a landscape, stopping and starting, pulled
towards a theory of unread sky—non-statements moving
past the usual preset and standardized textual demarcations
into dunes of words & rafts of collecting swerves, propelled
determinedly eastward. I think the only possible way
I could compose these poems, honoring my desire to lose
visual track of their origins to the left/west, is by typing
them into my internet browser bar, which might give me that
necessary past-blindness—the line disappearing into a formal
horizon as I move through the screen, making things
happen, or allowing their happening, as it may. I also enjoy
the potential conflict between what I foresee as the semi-
naturalist (ecopoetical?) leanings of these line curves and their

birth on the internet,
similar thing with a
paper. How have I not
draft, drift from a
of marks? Walk me
unavailable action.
kind of *happen*. I might
the word *here* and end the
more several. Something
in a frame. Razor clams.
swelling continent of bees.
Blue again.

pre-search. Archie Ammons did a
typewriter and coils of thin receipt
said causeway yet? How do you get,
theorized space to an arranged series
from pink to sandpiper along an
Grass escapes into itself. Pools just
want to start the first poem with
last poem with something a little
neither from nor towards. A body
Transferred moisture. Some
Far-off rocks rejecting light.
Something like that.

Fort Not

I'm not really that kind
of smart. Sometimes I can hardly.
I hear a little bell
and a film gets all over.

Twice yesterday, actually,
the imagined consensual entered.
Held onto for a long time. A shriek
parade was ordered by the county.

The gender I wanted to become
was actually more of an arm
movement—simultaneously
strong, accurate, elegant, lilting

and weaponized. Scrolling white text
opened doors to previous anticipation.
The opening credits came on last,
all puffed out with options.

I did this very gentle tapping
to activate the month in my skull.
I watched some massage-related porn
for purely relaxational purposes,

locked violets and crystals
in the gun safe. Mold bloomed
on the ceiling in the museum
of best practices. Everyone got sour.

If it's ok to cry
in this widening, groaning hall,
I'll do it after I sign
for the deliveries.

The smallest muscles in my hands
are hard at work
generating a closeness to god
that is rare in these parts.

When I end the American movie
and it rains all over the Puget Sound,
will you shepherd me
to the opposite of safety. Place

one hand at the small
of my wreck. Pour out
every single refreshment.
There's so many savings

and so little time.
Sally wore a bathing suit.
Nobody's home
at the Holiday Inn Express.

The scenic route drowned
a long time ago.
Didn't you know? Water froze
in the generation.

Fort Something

There was a history there of men overtaking and rebuilding and casting to ruin, then drawing up new plans, beginning anew, hesitating, revising only to tear down and build again, and always slightly off-center. The old structures lay low, shaven very close towards disappearing, and the men forgot what they had once been there for. They would pace the grounds, the current geometries and sketches leaving their minds the moment newer ones arrived. Neighboring cousins would ship in, ask to see the plans, squint at them, breathe heavily, muttering, "this needs to be done over," and a new process would start on top of forgotten plots, fresh visions interrupting and clotting over the preceding ones. Soon after the day the wrong stones (too smooth, or too flat, or not enough) were delivered for the second time, and a favorite work animal fell ill, interest in fortitude waned and the men scattered into neighboring projects, absorbing themselves with agriculture, family, and deep thought. The site had been abandoned for years when officials in England urged the nearby colony to rebuild against Native populations, citing their "growing hostility" and the location's military value. Colonel David Dunbar, Surveyor of His Majesty's Woods in America, took firm steps to reestablish a structure. Nobody was sure if there were beings watching from the woods, but the workers felt seen, then overseen, then ultimately neglected. They decided it would be best to construct around a giant rock, moved there and discarded like a bad egg by the Laurentide Ice Sheets, glaciers that traveled from

Canada 25,000 years earlier to sweep away much of the evidence of earlier glaciations, eroding both the bedrock and previously existing sediment cover. The boulder at the heart of the growing fort left little room inside for people or weapons or planning of any kind, only two small circular walkways connected by meager stairwells and a garret with no overhead or balustrade to speak of. Later, with the erection of Fort Pownall farther east and the fall of Quebec, the need for anything there ceased and the Massachusetts governor ordered the rebuilding to come to an end. The low walls of the ruins were, for a long time, used to house farming equipment. Then families began to come for picnics. Oyster shell heaps glowed underground, alkalizing the soil, never to be unearthed. A few vague and confusing plaques were posted and ignored. A preservation committee was formed and meets in the library on Tuesday evenings. Coffee is served with supermarket cake and the minutes are typed up by a secretary and sometimes lost. Just last week, two friends climbed to the top to take in the spectacular view. One wore red circular sunglasses and left them behind, hooked onto the newly installed guardrail. It is June 8th at sundown. It is the morning of June 9th. It is almost midday.

Alignment

On this day I have chosen place.

On this day with the sun and the wimpy field,
I eye a patch in the middle of the square
where the dry brown grass has not yet intruded.

The approach is nearly painless.
One foot, then the other, and so on,
until some might say I'm there.

A woman I've met many times waves
from the sidewalk in front of the bank,
but I do not wave. I remove my shoes,

though it seems someone else is doing this for me.

The transition from motion to motionlessness
is about release and alignment.

I think of the small circular movements of my pelvis,
the clenching of my hamstrings,
a twitch in my eyelid,
as the smallest deaths,

dissipating, winding down towards
the possibility of stillness, levitating it
like a yellow marble
behind my eye.

A predatory bird circles overhead
and a small round door
opens at the bottom of each of my heels.

Two metal screws emerge to begin
their deep descent into the earth below.

If you're wondering whether this hurts, it does.

And next there's this impenetrable enclosure
(picture a bulletproof aquarium, a cube)
it builds slowly around my body, filling
with a clear and wonderful liquid
that smells of paper and lavender and glue.

Another native bird with a red head
sticks its tiny pink tongue
into a pinecone in a nearby tree.

People begin to run towards me, shouting
from the periphery. This only accelerates

a process. I am not a man
on a horse. I am not a man with a sword.
I didn't put out any fires. The tide of resin
has reached my "widow's peak," which my first child
called my "little dark mountain," and will soon

encapsulate me. It's all very exciting.

If you worry about my breathing, don't.
Monuments breathe only pure movement
and glance. On this day I have chosen place.

This day with the sun and the wimpy field,
among idiots and liars and grotesque snobs,

and what I did and what I did not do.

And I say to this place, get used to me.
I have nothing left that didn't come from you.

Complete Set of Depression Glass

I'm afraid of hurting everybody no anybody.

In the house I drink only what pools in the smallest concavities.

The blue light is mine.
The tin cup. A drop.
A string horse.

A failing tree produces my replica.

I learned everything the hard way except nothing.

I learned it hardest leaning against a fence

Heart, glands in the roadway, weight
on one leg, ventilated
still and unchanging.

Any couch can see I'm afraid of doing.

I let things happen in a loose smock

moving on thought and want.

Tendrils of saliva fill the pod of the mouth.
The complaining terrain pounds the eye.
Conversations over bread replace the bread.

I get so relaxed it kills my whole family.

I might wear my flower suit into town. Perfume

the insides of my eyelids. What's easy isn't always visual.

The green and dirt will soon tear out the snow.

My friend picks me up in her new car. We drive

towards a still place inside the calendar year.

She leans across the console to say, "You should really stop tinkering
over the same old river,

the same one you'll call gray and the next day call gunmetal
the same one you'll drink from
the same one you'll cross

the same one you'll drown in

while you think you're being carried."

Girls Online

The first line is a row of girls,
twenty-five of them, almost
a painting, shoulders overlapping,
angled slightly towards you.
One says: *I'm myself here.*
The others shudder and laugh
through the ribbon core that strings
them. They make a tone tighter
by drumming on their thighs and
opening their mouths. The girls
are cells. The girls are a fence,
a fibrous network. One by one
they describe their grievances.
Large hot malfunctioning
machines lie obediently at their sides.
Their shirts are various shades
of ease in the surrounding air,
which is littered with small cuts.
One will choose you, press you
into the ground. You may never
recover. The second-to-last line
has a fold in it. The last line is
the steady pour of their names.

Poem with Orpheus

Every word in this poem is a dead body.
Each word dies as you read it
and floats behind in a wooden canoe
that covers itself with itself
to make a coffin. A white, historical plane
knits above the dead word to shroud
and replace it. The poem before (this) point
is streaming and invisible. The rivulets
on which the coffin boats float
move backwards forever. That last word (word)
and then (last) (that) (forever) (backwards)
(move)—you killed those words.
You actually wrote this poem in its own blood.
The poem was alive just a minute ago
and then you arrived. You walked (here)
sluggishly against the wind of the underworld
to push against each heavy body. I'm trying
to (protect) these (words) (from) you (with)
((special armor)). If you view this entire poem
in a mirror you will see death at work
as you see bees behind glass in a hive.
That last line is from Cocteau's *Orphée,*
a film in which we come to know
all poems are direct transmissions
from the dead. When I transcribed it I reversed

its screen death and then (((you))) came
and looked at it, sending it back
to this blank page, a banal trauma,
a repeated rest on nothing.

Crystal Radio

I am left here with an atmosphere of encounter
pressuring a surface in me. See you later.
There is too much afternoon on a plate, too much
Exit Preparedness. It's better right here by the open

valve. The internet gives birth whenever I go to her,
small wet caves rushing from her mouth into the data-
plushness of whatever room I designed that day. In my alone
time there are containers of Blank Element to disturb,

places to go with my skirt lifted way way up.
An unplugged speaker blasts your name into a basement.
I've noticed that the mechanism you need to get
at sensation floats by just as you think of it, shimmers

and is quieted. This is my decanter of too many samples, too many
furtive utterances. I do it because I love to empty the moment.
An opening orange squirts a lot of stuff onto a decorative seashell.
I was never here. I'm not coming back. I'm at sea.

Chalky Undertaste

if you majored in art and depressed lunch
please tell me where to put my right foot
at the exact moment I realize I'm repeating
myselves and please tell me where to
put it down

in the courtyard watching
art thicken and disassemble in the light
bits of tree come in diagonals
to translate paint
over layers of wet text clicking

the image was soggy, pointless, sans garland
staring at a town without bathing
or activist procedural guides, not even
a communal tear depository
for Big Suckers

everything kind of a muskless wash
a limp statue, no knowable tone
paper on paper announced dead
a bowl of micro-finches
poured over semiotics

the color pulled tightly around the word
and then loosened—pastel, chalk in the dye,
peachly, grains in the eye, lacking essential
saturation, afternoon cream,
chicken water

noting the drainage charts of male desire
young women slouched
to get their borders just right
young vegetables
loved to the best of their ability

this recurring sensation
a little perched doughnut
gathers dryly inside

the doughnut is loss

I untouch you
and move headfirst into the couches
of this unholy season

Emily Brontë's Last Words

Oh it's me we're looking at
& we're looking at it together.
I'm lounging on some kind of pixel

ated lawn chair. I'm the color
of pewter melting
over a bucket of peonies.

This is obviously upside down:
the image baffling
the domestic circuitry.

You can see my girl
organs through my skin,
which (the whole

surface) is constantly streaming
Truffaut's *Two English Ladies*.
It's a humiliating and rare condition.

My legs have an opening
mechanism. Whiteout
springs to the unkempt thigh.

I speak the weather to you.
You speak it back. Lovely
outer coinage—how we go all

sincere. I see hegemony as
a hammock swinging overhead
filled with catalogues;

every once in a while
one falls down & hits you
on the workerbrain.

Am I the furniture,
or the pattern,
resting plaintively, on it?

Upholstery
is the stepdaughter
of surface.

This replayed scene reveals
the tiniest ever pink
cactus in the shop window.

Give me it. That moonflower
we talked about, high
on the air arc. Give it here.

I stole all those tools
you used on me
& bloomed them.

Sisters or not,
if you send for a doctor
I will see him now.

Gel

I feel sick.
I feel very sick.
I feel very sick all the time.
Many have observed this,
but I am saying it now—
that packaged
with an experience of me
as a person is also
the experience of hearing me
tell you the ways
in which things feel
not at all right
at any given moment.
For instance,
there are these aching gaps
where my fingernails end,
where outer space intrudes
as punishing meaning,
rushing towards an alcove
of inner ease. Form is
a muscle weakening
around my limbs. Could you
speak a little louder?
There is this small, metallic
churning in my left ear.

Been there years.
No foods sustain me.
I shake at odd hours.
Trees, whipping about,
hurt my teeth, as does even
the most genial applause,
which I have complained about
since childhood—a marriage
of praiseworthy performance
with pain in the jaw—so that
early in the formation
of memories, classical music
became associated with
an ache nobody else
understood. I take
my earrings out.
They still feel in.
When I'm at a party
I feel sickest
because of the curators.
When I ask the people my age
what they do
it gets all vague and funny,
until I'm catching
huge chunks
of sterile cotton in midair
and applying them to
my sores and scabs.

The jungle's wallpaper
knocks my eyes
out of alignment. No day
exists where I do not vomit
or think about vomiting,
initiated by motion or
its opposite, the inability
to move or decide, a paralysis
brought on by the glimmering
bounty of the everyday. The world
ends in a big flash
on the screen of my desiring
forehead and a gel of pictures
pours out of my ass.
The recurring feeling
of falling through the base
of my skull and pooling
in my own shoes. My skin
is growing very thick,
a thickness that extends
towards outside affinities
as if to shake hands, like an
ill-equipped shoreline,
not a thickness that acts
as a barrier,
not one that makes me safe.
I've never gotten at

what's good and what's not
but I think I know
that the opposite
of the Yiddish proverb
is truer. Better to have
a beautiful hole
than an ugly patch.
"You love that dirty,
off-gold color,"
he says to me
looking at my hands
and big, decaying purse
which are full of it
and trembling
(is trembling always
bad)
I think it's not that.
I think I like the very clean
gold the perfect kind
that comes from love
and approaching a source
and there I am
collecting it and
making it mine
then something happens
something awful
again and again.

Fort Not

      Don't send money
      Don't send thoughts
      Don't send flowers to die
on my table
      Don't send form
      Don't send goods
      Don't send space
      Don't send the sensual
      Don't send energy, eccentricity
anything living
      Don't send credit
      Don't send ideas
please for the love of god don't send the body
      Don't send creation
      Don't send image
curation
no gender
      Don't send design
      Don't send metaphor
      Don't send design your own
      Don't send the account
      Don't send a collective
or individual action
      Don't send art
      Don't send clean lines

Don't send investment
Don't send activism
Don't send the flag, the obelisk
Don't send your shitty living rooms
they all look alike
Don't send perspective
Don't send context
Don't send history
Don't send influence
the hot object
Don't send movement
Don't send craft
habit
tendency
the soft myth
architecture
that shirt in the window
Don't send it
Don't send the song either
Don't send love
Don't send progress
Don't send poetry, no
Don't send a home
Don't send friends, no
they've all gone anyway
Send
Send   water
Send   thing

Send   color
         texture

Send   the dirt
Send   nothing

Send   sound

Send   death
Then sound again

c/o

you take one down c/o
another you take one
you take it down

take one down c/o
through another you take it
record one c/o things

c/o border c/o relation
you receive c/o the other
you get it, it comes

c/o you the you c/o you
the letter c/o the taken down
the vanished, the ousted

you take one down c/o
another you take it in
it attaches c/o other
you feel it, though it's through
another, c/o them in you

there is placement c/o line
alignment c/o signal
the names are c/o recordings, records
you've taken down
you take the letter down
c/o one another
you pull one, reroute it
bring it down by way of
alternate passage

the fractured letter
with the bite taken out
the letter that's a bay,
a fleshy grip, a toy claw

a name that's a pool
an enclosure a green
soap dish a Petri dish
the frontal word
pushing through
against teeth
to escape you

you take me down through
a different system of delivery
c/o indirect address
c/o gesture
thrown against into gaze

c/o pause, the hands pulled
apart c/o the shoulder blades
c/o fascia c/o the cord the impulse

what intensity c/o hands
hands caring carving over
almost humming
cauterization of the present
care of you

you take one down
to consider it
one stopping cold, paused
a remainder alone removed

care of one, for one, one for one
one though one, one through one
care of an other, one another

you take one down c/o
another you take one
you take it down

tender abbreviation
you shut it down
in me, sweetly in me
you blur it away inside the line in me

Basement Delivery

Having lived so long without one, we forgot
what a basement felt like—how it seemed
to the carriers, to the inhabitants,
the structures, that there was an *underneathness*
to all that daily interaction and exchange—
i.e. an empty teacup hovering just above a pool.

On the day the basement was delivered,
pink air made its way underneath the canopy.
Ten strong women arrived to pump it through the ground,
evicting domestic earthworms, telepathic moss
and scarce minerals. An important rivulet was rerouted.
The sub-story attached and crystallized like in that dream.

The whole procedure only took a few minutes.
In the presence of a basement, our history was whisked,
indexed into a ladder, roped down—our kidneys and lungs
wrung out. We stood around slowly. We were cooled
and stored. In the parlor, at first blush of waking,
our usual words and arrangements seemed normal enough,

but then that lower sound, that kept air, funneled up to us.
A collection freed itself. It was *again* again. Leave no stone already.

Carpet Town

I walked into the ugly carpet
and decided to live there.
Everyone was there already,
all the cats I ever loved, my favorite sodas
and snack cakes,
most of my friends and family.
Their names were slightly altered,
but only by a few letters,
and they were people I loved
and recognized. I wasn't worried.
I found a warm spot on the southeast corner
near the puke green stripe
and settled in
really got comfortable
with the tinny sounds
and the body soil
and the faint feet smell
and this squeaking sound like grass weeping
whenever you moved or someone greeted you
with a wave or deep bow.
And I was in love with the way the carpet
held you in place, inside a delightful,
straightjacket tightness.
I enjoyed
the way the green and red fibers

almost mixed at my border
but didn't. It made me remember
segmented fields of flowers.
I was sad for a minute and missed nature.
I started a lucrative dish delivery service
for people who needed more dishes
or just wanted new ones.
Then something really weird started to happen.
All of my friends' faces, the people I knew
from before my carpet days,
from tongue red and assfoam,
spirulina, and Marmite beige,
grew metal faces. They had been dipped
by something, held by the feet
and lowered into a vat.
Their gestures made eerie sounds.
They stopped talking. I was scared.
The carpet loosened around us.
I grabbed my favorite dishes
and hid inside a fiber loop
long enough to catch my breath.
It was getting dark as I began to wonder
where I might put my face to sleep.
I walked until I reached the edge.
I could hear the low howls of the dead.
The cats had followed me.
I always do dumb shit like this.

Daything

I could attract a method if I sat still long enough
and opened to various mouths of influence.

Mind rerouted because of some edge or atomic chain
and the way a noisy petal bursts to my eye. Sob!

Maybe this is why I identify with decorative bowls—afternoons
of dust and nothing, waiting to never receive. Honey

instruments. A word that moves on the ground its whole life,
leaving trails of mucus, collecting parts, dying in secret.

Ideally there would be no spectators. There might be bodies
softly threatening against documents of installed idiocy.

I subscribe to the privatized drinking water, click boxes,
make futile mating calls to precision, logic, emotional

maturity, biodiversity, rationality and informed decision-making.
I respond to an email, another arrives to replace it.

The subaqueous rummaging of all that's heavy and beautiful.
The seasick mouthful. The hardening problem. Hands retreat
    from memory

foam. Rising ocean temperatures already killing plankton
    necessary
to support all marine life. Whales underneath everything said.

Tapering clouds wring like sponges onto a conversational valley.
There's gum in the jaws of a participating half of a tender embrace.

Narratives trample onto patios—Suffering. Precipice. Love.
Empathy. Betrayal. Anger. Anger. Betrayal. Precipice. Anger.

Betrayal. Suffering. Love. Anger. Suffering. Precipice. Nature.
Empathy. Strategy. Color. Suffering. Something like love. I try
    to write

"I feel the same" in response to a confession, but mistype
"I feel the sand." Sunburned on a stupid beach of zero ideas.

A logic grows, a white chrysanthemum.
It becomes very intense and external, like opera.

Ultrasound in Virgo

"There is a right anterior upper uterine transmural fibroid
measuring 4.5 x 4.2 x 3.3 cm. Previously this measured
3 x 2.4 x 2.8 cm."

—WEST SIDE RADIOLOGY, APRIL 21, 2017

I reached down into the pot
of sunset fragments,
took a handful
to spread on the reticulum

vacated a painting
with a hiss, for another
with TV, a man, that mushroom
lamp, a good tree

you crossed the room
I took no food. The air
carried a message
a scheme dropped

to its fours
heat constellating
through the old body
its door of life

when I exhaled in bed
the sound surprised me
someone else trapped, held
in time, her songs escaped

"I'm in pain," I say
to the technician
spray of continuation
little net of memory

(her hand bears down)
what use have you
you there in the water
why wail to us?

Parallelogram

A muted video of two clean white women mouthing "lifestyle."
They approach a produce cart, one sniffs an orange
and full-smiles, one a holds a quartered watermelon
with both hands and hunches over to put her grinning face to it
like it's the National Chosen Thing.
The smiles/sniffs aren't in perfect step, but flow
over each other's unique timing like a double-pour
into the ideal combined face. They hold hands
over dirty radishes, gently finger swaths
of multicolored lettuce, and squint
into a microbiome sun. One says "inside out,"
and a pink cartoon colon materializes between them.

I've named the women Peggy and Polly
because they are obviously cultural twins, just different
enough to allow for variations in stripe thickness
on a linen shirt or exact pupillary distance.
A slightly rounded front tooth glints from their daytime
into my surrounding night, where I sit in my own territory
of acute bedding, letting pictures dart at brain
and throat and domes of cartilage.
And what do you know one second Peggy's Polly
the next Polly's Peggy. So (rattled)
I minimize the window that has opened between us
and take the dog's photo and move books from one room

to another. Just last week Milla serenaded me over the phone
with a composition of impressively accurate puffin calls,
low groany honks, lamenting her choice
to produce these same sounds in a moment of panic
for Pinky, a prospective male lover at the TV studio
where they are mutually employed. I told her
about the "slow release" method of dating, a capsule-based
recommendation to issue your personality to another
in small, border-blended increments, like *picture your identity
as coated in a porous and slowly dissolving barrier.*
It wears away and you hand yourself over, secrete gestures
and sounds from your core into their dull receptacle.

The only thing I can do is write poems
for those who'd like me vaporized. A woman on another coast
writes public notes I think are about me
because I am fucking her beloved. She writes
he should be embarrassed, and I think of my humiliation
as a badge, a subterranean violet gas gaining volume
and beauty. Her poems are sparse and sad and plain,
like natural occurrences under blue light
in one of the more mountainous states, and I often think
"you can have him," and consider that maybe it is her I want
and that we've created, in our mutual and aligned upset,
a transcontinental bile pipeline to transport horrors of our love.

I suspect I am irrevocably vain and demented
and that people can sense this but I see no way out
other than to keep touching her, my sister in sadness,
through the screen with my weathered thumb.
I'm becoming obsessed with a woman I've never met
I write my Upper East Side therapist. I watch a video
of a goat dying and another goat mourning it by bowing
its head and chest to the ground. I watch a video of a small girl
terrified of her own shadow, one where the beauty
of synchronized movement collapses into a horrible accident,
and another in which a procession of Highplains white-tails
cross the bluest water ever seen, moving shore

to shore with a calm that should probably solve something
but doesn't. As a young girl, I devised a makeshift pet
by keeping a bowl of water in my room and refilling it fresh
every few days, and I'm not clear if the bowl was the pet
or if the pet was the water or some combination of the two,
but it was something I cared for against days and weeks
of loneliness. So now I'm here, she's over there,
and then we cross to switch places. Now I'm still "here,"
and she I suppose is "over there." How odd
after all that walking. And one second Peggy's Polly
the next Polly's Peggy as expected. Something inherits me
and I go straight to it without hesitation, the way

one adjustable square of experience covers another, then disappears.
The last time I was late it was to a class about women and writing.
The last time I felt happy I was vacuuming and blew a fuse.
The last time I went somewhere new
it was only two hours away and not very good.
Tomorrow, earlyish, I might purchase a century's worth
of cut fruit and arrange it across the table
in the hopes of ushering in some new state
of thinking and embodiment, but as of now, right now,
these two blondes I trust are leaning a flower against
its neighboring flower, and telling me that with their help
my skin will start to glow.

Bay

I feel a *ness*ness
and it grows
in color and size
until I can no longer sit
obediently at my tulip
table in my boiled shirt
and my bursting polish
counting my blanks and fews
until I leap up in eight
thousand uncalculated motions
one more jagged than the next
like a fistful of weapons aimed
at getting nothing done
in a subject clouding over
and come to a momentary sill

I feel a *ness*ness
and something is ready
towards the core of it
to be drawn out and placed
into vials and a network of paper strips
marked with fine tip instruments
and presented before a court
that is tasked with determining
the weight we beat upon each other

and the burden on the air and small
creatures that must be, copper ounce
by ounce, lifted by the uptick
of our sternums, mid-haul
the troubling
vapors filling a repository
ordinary sound embalms us inside

I feel a *ness*ness
but what to do with the exchange
of funds required to numb our
erosion, the late-night fidget of numbers
hemorrhaging into a surrounding white
I went into the woods with some friends
we built a fire with nutritional pamphlets
I came out a movement of bright spots
pressed to a retreating shadow
the light on the little bush
at the edge of the property
made it look or seem to shake
witnessing the feelings of others
in the heat's color, a jealousy
developed bluely—toxic little center

I feel a *ness*ness
I never arrive and nobody
tells me a thing
as if I could be more arc than stamp

a platter with scented branches
smudge at the tip of thought
the creaking dock from which
the boats of me sail off
fine folk, ghosts, friends,
I ask for delicate activation
I need it to live and breathe, to go on
to leave. How do you know you know,
you know? I have no more room
to lay down in this life. This light
on my hand becomes my hand

Champion Flowers

I hope this note finds you feeling very comfortable.
I'm in the fourth antechamber on the right,
just trying something new on the picture.
There are buckets of color for our advancement—
amassed lilies make a green cave. Lightest sardines
tossed against dishwater light. Duplicate birds.
I caught a swelling node. How? It can happen.
Buildings grow along the timeline like bacterial crystals.
I found the wildest circles to shade through.
I admit I stressed about it, but it was productive.
It could be finished early as tomorrow.

In the daily revision everything gets toned way
way down. I feel squashed, but tell myself to power
around, metallic and thin, throw out the gaudy textiles.
The mold toxicity results arrive under the door.
It would be presumptive to say the dreariness of outside
will leave us feeling determined and invigorated.
The word format is gone. The word dwelling
disappears. The wall dissolves into a pile.
Just like that, as they often say.

I dim the Himalayan salt lamp. Nothing goes here.
I've tried almost everything. We let ourselves outside.
But now, doused in your new black felt cape, you look better

than ever before, bending to admire the gray rocks.
We make a blue line in the field with our breath.
Could this be diagrammed? I fear I am always tired.
You returning your back to me, a swivel
into a predetermined groove. I couldn't get
that texture back after that day. It was gone.
Is a report possible? It is impossible.

Grateful acknowledgement is made to the editors of the following journals and online publications in which many of these poems first appeared:

Big Lucks, BOMB, Boston Review, Brooklyn Rail, Conduit, Gramma, Hyperallergic, iO: A Journal of New American Poetry, jubilat, LitHub, Maggy, Open House, Phantom Limb, Philadelphia Review of Books, Pleiades, Academy of American Poets *Poem-a-Day, POETRY, Poor Claudia :: Crush, Riot of Perfume, The The Poetry,* and *Washington Square.*

Some of these poems appeared in *Backchannel,* a chapbook published by Poor Claudia in 2014.

"Baby Food" and "Fort Not" were included in in the Brooklyn Poets Anthology, edited by Jason Koo and Joe Pan.

"Basement Delivery" appeared in the 2017 Pushcart Prize Anthology.

"Chalky Undertaste" was printed as a poster-sized broadside with Krystal Languell's chapbook, *Fashion Blast Quarter,* by Flying Object in Hadley, Massachusetts.

With immense gratitude to my editors, Ben Estes and Alan Felsenthal, who made the process of publishing my first book an incredible experience.

Thank you

to my teachers: Dorothea Lasky, Timothy Donnelly, Cathy Park Hong, Richard Howard, Alberto Manguel, and Jennifer Firestone for your guidance, insight, and support;

to Lois and Jim Skillings;

to Danniel Schoonebeek;

to Samantha Zighelboim, Milla Bell-Hart, Ali Power, Marcella Durand, Adam Fitzgerald, Claudia Rankine, Simone Kearney, Tan Lin, Eileen Myles, John Ashbery, David Kermani, Wendy Xu, Krystal Languell, Nina Puro, Rachel Levitsky, Chia-Lun Chang, erica kaufman, Caroline Crumpacker, Zachary Pace, Eric Dean Wilson, Travis Meyer, Allyson Paty, Will Brewer, Ryann Stevenson, Farnoosh Fathi, Sara Joy Márquez, Dara Cerv, xtian w, Oli Hazzard, Elizabeth Hazan, Katie Raissian, Christopher Russell, Ava Lehrer, Ricardo Maldonado, Karin Roffman, Jimin Seo, Bianca Stone, Ivy Johnson, Jamie Townsend, Stacey Tran, Jonah Rosenberg, Tom Healy, Todd Colby, Sasha Litvinov, Mónica de la Torre, Rich Smith, Alex Kennedy-Grant, Tyler Weston Jones, CA Kaufman, Granny, Gregory Scheidler, Megan and Eric Bosarge, Katie and Ben

Grant, Heidi Esterman, Jessamee Sanders, Zach Whitney, Katie Turner, Cheryl Rust, and Alexandra Beller;

to my classmates at the Columbia University MFA program for writing alongside me;

to the Steven Arnold archive;

to the feminists of Belladonna★ Collaborative.